THE HEYDAY OF MAIDSTONE & DISTRICT

Ian Allan
PUBLISHING

Glyn Kraemer-Johnson and John Bishop

Front cover: Looking smart following a repaint and with polished radiator is all-Leyland Titan PD2/12 DH402 (NKT 898), turning into Lower Stone Street bus station *en route* to Hastings. Taken during the summer of 1967, the photograph shows a piece of transport history unfolding — the rapid dismantling of the overhead for Maidstone's trolleybuses, which had been withdrawn en masse on 15 April; in the background can be seen one of their diesel-engined replacements, a Massey-bodied Leyland Atlantean in Maidstone Corporation's then-new livery of pale blue and cream. Note also the Lambretta scooter and the pillion passenger with no crash helmet, which would be unheard of today. *Dave Brown*

Back cover: New in 1946 as a conventional single-decker, Beadle-bodied AEC Regal SO16 (HKL 826) was one of three converted to open-top in 1957/8. The example seen here was renumbered as OR2 upon conversion in November 1957 and then again as 8002 in 1968, becoming 4002 in 1975. By September 1976, when this photograph was taken in Hastings, the vast majority of the fleet had donned NBC leaf green, so it was especially pleasing that the open-top AEC Regals were allowed to retain traditional livery. The surviving pair (the third having been sold in 1971) would pass to Hastings & District in 1983, but happily all three are now lovingly cared for in preservation. Note in the background the cliff lift, still a feature of Hastings. *John Bishop / Online Transport Archive*

Title page: A scene which epitomises Maidstone & District bus operation in rural Kent. Bound for Tunbridge Wells on route 97, DH398 (NKT 894), an all-Leyland PD2/12 dating from 1951, trundles through the sparsely populated countryside near Rolvenden in the spring of 1967. Little wonder that Kent is known as the 'Garden of England'. *Dave Brown*

Left: In the period 1958-63 M&D took delivery of some 147 Leyland Atlanteans. New in 1963 as DH627, Weymann-bodied 5627 (627 UKM) is seen at the side of the old East Kent garage in Rye in March 1976; note the NBC-sponsored 'Save It' advertisements. Although the Atlantean design facilitated one-man operation (legalised for double-deckers in 1966), M&D's large fleet was not converted for OMO until the early 1970s, this particular example being adapted in May 1972. *John Bishop / Online Transport Archive*

First published 2006

ISBN (10) 0 7110 3115 0
ISBN (13) 978 0 7110 3115 9

All rights reserved. No part of this book may be reproduced or transmitted in any form or by any means, electronic or mechanical, including photocopying, recording or by any information storage and retrieval system, without permission from the Publisher in writing.

© Ian Allan Publishing 2006

Published by Ian Allan Publishing

an imprint of Ian Allan Publishing Ltd, Hersham, Surrey KT12 4RG.
Printed in England by Ian Allan Printing Ltd, Hersham, Surrey KT12 4RG.

Code: 0605/B2

Visit the Ian Allan Publishing website at www.ianallanpublishing.com

Introduction

They were like three sisters: three sisters who ruled the South East for more than 50 years. One was dignified, immaculately dressed, a cut above the rest. Her name was Southdown. Then there was pretty little East Kent, the shy one, who went efficiently about her business disturbing no one. The third sister was more butch, down-to-earth, no frills. She had a job to do, and she went about it regardless of whether it might make her paintwork dusty. She was Maidstone & District.

With the exception of one Tilling-group company, three municipalities and a handful of independents, these three subsidiaries of the British Electric Traction Group (BET) between them operated the bus services in Kent, Sussex and part of Hampshire. Maidstone & District's territory was sandwiched between the other two, its operating area including the Kent county town of Maidstone from which it took its name and in which was situated Knightrider House, its Head Office. The 'District' extended from the southern banks of the Thames estuary to the Sussex coast. Having absorbed the services of Chatham & District, M&D became the sole operator in the Medway towns of Rochester, Gillingham, Strood and Chatham, the latter with its famous Naval dockyard, then fully operational. It served the Isle of Sheppey with its seaside resorts of Sheerness and Leysdown and the North Kent market towns of Sittingbourne and Faversham, the latter being the boundary with East Kent. It ran through the orchards and the hop-fields of mid-Kent, it carried all those 'disgusteds' from Tunbridge Wells and reached the Sussex coast at Rye and Hastings. Jointly with Southdown it ran from there to Eastbourne and from Tunbridge Wells as far west as Brighton. With East Kent it reached Folkestone and Canterbury in the east. In Hastings it became one of the few BET companies to operate trolleybuses, initially retaining the Hastings Tramways fleetname and then under its own title, *The* Maidstone & District Motor Services Ltd; there was no other.

**Introduction by Glyn Kraemer-Johnson
Photographs selected and captioned
by John Bishop**

In 1944/5 M&D took delivery of no fewer than 63 Bristol K6As, with utility bodywork. Rebodied by Weymann in 1953, DH159 (HKE 867) continued in service until 1967, when it was sold direct into preservation with the Maidstone & District and East Kent Bus Club. This photograph — taken in Brighton in May 1974, on the occasion of the Historic Commercial Vehicle Club's annual London–Brighton run — shows the horizontal light-green lining which so enhanced the livery but which was discontinued in the 1950s as an economy measure. Note too the East Kent Leyland Titan PD1 (CJG 959), also in the ownership of the M&D and East Kent Bus Club.
John Bishop / Online Transport Archive

Left: Among the more unusual vehicles purchased by M&D were 15 Harrington-bodied Albion Nimbuses, for use on lightly trafficked rural routes. This view features preserved SO308 (308 LKK), operating a free service as part of the Hastings Running Day of 10 October 1992. *John Bishop*

Left: Also taking part in the 1992 Hastings Running Day was one-time M&D SO43 (LKT 991), one of a batch of 16 standard-length ECW-bodied Bristol L6As delivered in 1950. Since the photograph was taken the railway station has been completely rebuilt. *John Bishop / Online Transport Archive*

Right: In 1951 Maidstone & District purchased its flagship vehicle, LC1 (NKN 650), a Harrington-bodied Commer Avenger always known by its name, *The Knightrider*. The specification would befit any luxury car of the time, with bar facilities, tables and reversible seating for just 16 people. The vehicle remained with M&D, retaining its distinctive dark-blue livery and even its Commer petrol engine, throughout the NBC era, being seen at a rally at Wittersham Road (near the Kent & East Sussex Railway) in August 1981. Sold following the company's change of ownership in the late 1990s, it remains lovingly cared for today. *John Bishop / Online Transport Archive*

M&D's livery of dark green and cream was perhaps not as pretty as Southdown's apple green or East Kent's cherry red (how appropriate for the area!) but was attractive nonetheless. Originally lined out in a lighter shade of green, its double-deckers were distinguished by a silver roof, and all its vehicles carried that marvellous 'scroll' fleetname. Underfloor-engined single-deckers and rear-engined double-deckers were adorned with what became known as the M&D 'moustache' — a cream-painted

area below the windscreen that had originally been a feature of Harrington-bodied single-deckers and coaches.

For single-deckers and coaches Maidstone & District was a staunch supporter of local bodybuilders Beadle of Dartford and, in particular, Thomas Harrington of Hove. In the 'Thirties the company even bought some Harrington-bodied double-deckers — rare birds indeed. In its choice of chassis it was more liberal than its sisters, taking large numbers of

AECs, Leylands, Guys, Bristols, Daimlers and Commers, as well as 'one-offs' such as a Saro integral single-decker and *The Knightrider* — the well-known petrol-engined Commer Avenger with Harrington 'executive' coachwork, painted in a livery of all-over dark blue.

M&D was one of the first operators to purchase the rear-engined Leyland Atlantean, which it used to replace the Hastings trolleybuses and then went on to take large numbers with Metro-Cammell

5

and Weymann 'Orion'-style bodywork of both highbridge and lowbridge layout. In the authors' eyes they looked hideous when first delivered but have improved with time — or have our attitudes softened? The company had earlier carried out a massive rebodying programme of Guy, Bristol and Daimler wartime utility double-deckers, mostly with Weymann bodies, many of which were to the Orion lightweight design.

Along with the other BET companies M&D became part of the National Bus Company on 1 January 1969, ultimately losing its traditional livery of dark green and cream in favour of an uninspiring leaf green and white, the coaches adopting an even less inspiring all-over white. Ties with East Kent were strengthened during the NBC period, culminating in the introduction of a common fleet-numbering scheme, and for a while it looked as though the two companies might be merged. This did not happen, however, and in November 1986 Maidstone & District was subject to a management buy-out, becoming one of the first NBC companies to be privatised. The new company adopted a livery of leaf green and cream that was not too dissimilar to that of neighbouring Southdown. In 1995 Maidstone & District was bought by British Bus, one of several groups that were busily acquiring management-owned companies. British Bus launched what must have been one of the most attractive liveries we had seen in many a year. Basically a dark emerald green and cream applied to a traditional layout, it introduced a simplified version of the famous M&D scroll fleetname. The result was superb. Alas, it was short-lived. British Bus sold out to the Cowie group, which in turn became Arriva, the fleet duly adopted the now-familiar livery of 'shimmering aquamarine and Cotswold stone', and the Maidstone & District name disappeared along with 86 years of tradition.

In this volume we have included a selection of photographs intended to illustrate the wide variety of buses and coaches operated by the company and the contrasting backcloth against which they worked. The majority are, naturally enough, from the days of BET ownership, but there are a few from the NBC-owned and privatised company, which round off the story. M&D has a strong following amongst bus enthusiasts and is fondly remembered by those living in the area it served.

We hope this book will rekindle memories of the days when the operator serving west Kent and much of East Sussex was The Maidstone & District Motor Services.

Glyn Kraemer-Johnson
Hailsham, East Sussex
March 2006

Left: Three years after its formation (in 1969) NBC introduced its corporate image, M&D adopting leaf-green livery. Following privatisation in November 1986 the company set about creating a new identity, retaining the well-respected name but with a new fleetname style and the white waistband replaced by a subtle shade of cream. This April 1988 view of 1972 Leyland Leopard/Marshall 3456 (EKL 456K) — coincidentally the last vehicle delivered in traditional livery — descending Mount Pleasant Road in Tunbridge Wells shows immediately the improvement afforded by these two simple alterations. *John Bishop / Online Transport Archive*

Left: Enthusiasts would never have dreamed that when the privatised Maidstone & District was purchased by British Bus the National green used hitherto would give way to such a stylish new livery. Bathed in perfect sunlight at Battle while *en route* for Hastings, Bristol VR/ECW 5883 (HKM 883V) displays the new-style fleetname suggesting the 'Heyday' has started all over again! Alas it was not to last; British Bus would shortly become part of the Cowie group, and M&D's handsome new livery would give way to the Arriva corporate image. *Dave Brown*

Right: In 2005 Stagecoach repainted Hastings & District Volvo B10M/Northern Counties 20654 (R654 HCD) into full M&D livery, complete with scroll fleetname and even a depot plate on the rear, to mark the 100th anniversary of Hastings trams. The lettering to this effect had still to be applied when the photograph was taken at the Magnificent Motors rally in Eastbourne on 1 May, so the bus looked correct for the purposes of this book! A similar vehicle was painted in Hastings Tramways maroon and cream. *John Bishop / Online Transport Archive*

Left: New in 1939 as 295 and renumbered in 1950, Leyland Titan TD5/Weymann open-topper OT1 (FKO 225) was one of a batch of six such vehicles which for many years looked set to be the last purpose-built open-toppers (as opposed to convertibles or permanent conversions from closed-top buses) delivered in the UK. It is seen here in Battle High Street, in the early 1960s in the company of Park Royal-bodied AEC Regent V DH477 (VKR 469). Also worthy of mention is the Commer Cob (left), as are the two intending customers (right) trying to decide whether to rent one of the television sets on display. *Howard Butler*

Right: A Bristol K6A delivered in 1944, DH111 (HKE 212) started life with wartime utility bodywork by Park Royal but was rebodied by Weymann in 1951 after chassis refurbishment, thereby gaining a 14-year life extension. It is seen in the early 1960s at Overcliffe, Gravesend. Behind is S201 (UKN 201), one of the Harrington-Commer integral single-deck buses delivered in 1955, while in the background are the tops of the cranes for unloading vessels docked in the Thames Estuary. *Howard Butler*

Right: A Bristol K6A delivered in 1945 sporting a Park Royal utility body, DH128 (HKE 229) was enhanced by the fitting in 1953 of the handsome Weymann body seen in this early-1960s view at St John's Road garage in Tunbridge Wells. Worthy of note is the autovac (beneath the nearside front window) to draw the fuel from the diesel tank to the engine, also a feature of prewar Leyland Titan and Tiger models. *Malcolm Keeping*

Left: Taking more than an hour from end to end, route 79 linked Uckfield and Tunbridge Wells via Buxted, Hadlow Down and Mayfield. Seen outside the old Southdown garage at Uckfield in the early 1960s, DH122 (HKE 223), a Weymann-rebodied Bristol K6A, enjoys a rest before departing on the short working to Buxted, which ran every two hours. *Malcolm Keeping*

Above: Uckfield on a thoroughly gloomy day in the mid-1960s is the venue for DH160 (HKE 868), a Bristol K6A delivered in 1945 with a utility Duple body and rebodied by Weymann in 1953. The bus is seen on the lengthy route 122 to Gravesend, which journey — judging by the remains of snow on the bus-station roof — would have been a cold experience. It is fascinating to note that a packet of 20 cigarettes cost just under 20 pence. Note also (right) the prewar Model Y Ford blocking the bus-station concourse. *Malcolm Keeping*

11

Left: Seen at Overcliffe, Gravesend, where many vehicles used to lay over between duties, is Bristol K6A DH130 (HKE 231) delivered in 1945. New with a Park Royal utility body, this vehicle was another of its type to be rebodied by Weymann, in this case in 1954 to that builder's later 'Orion' style. Behind is Park Royal-bodied AEC Reliance S266 (266 DKT), dating from 1959. *Howard Butler*

Right: Two for the price of one. This view, recorded in Maidstone's Mill Street bus station in the early 1960s, shows the marked differences between the Weymann bodies on DH134 and 159 (HKE 235, 867). Both based on Bristol K6A chassis delivered in 1945, they would soldier on in rebodied form until 1967. Route 5, which linked Gillingham and Hastings via Maidstone, still operates in truncated form between Maidstone and Hastings, while DH159 survives in preservation with the Maidstone & District and East Kent Bus Club and is a regular sight at rallies. *Howard Butler*

Right: Maidstone & District garages were in the main very functional buildings, as apparent from this mid-1960s view of Station Road garage in Ashford, playing host to three 1945 Bristol K6As rebodied in the early 1950s by Weymann. From left to right are DH159, 123 and 114 (HKE 867, 224, 215). On the far right is Weymann-bodied AEC Reliance S329 (329 NKT), dating from 1961. *Howard Butler*

Left: After the war M&D continued to favour Bristol chassis and in 1948 purchased no fewer than 40 handsome Weymann-bodied K6As, including DH255 (KKK 861), seen in Southborough High Street on local route 98 to Ramslye Estate in Tunbridge Wells. The letters 'K' and 'M' on either side of the destination display, constituting an advertisement for the *Kent Messenger* newspaper, were a common feature of M&D buses in the 1950s and '60s. *Malcolm Keeping*

Below left: Another photograph taken at Mill Street bus station, Maidstone, in the early 1960s, this time a close-up of 1945 Daimler CWA6 DH46 (HKE 282) rebodied by Weymann in 1953. Its long service was due in part to the then-standard AEC engine as used in M&D's large fleet of Bristols, represented here by DH118 (HKE 219), itself rebodied by Weymann in 1954. The application of *Kent Messenger* advertisements is again apparent. *Howard Butler*

14

This view at Mill Street bus station, Maidstone, in the early 1960s shows the marked difference between lowbridge and highbridge vehicles as well as the fleet-numbering system used by Maidstone & District, which is logic in itself. The letters 'DH' denote double-deck highbridge and 'DL' double-deck lowbridge, as carried (left) by DL22 (LKT 983), a Weymann-bodied Bristol K6A of 1950. Next to it is DH48 (HKE 284), a 1945 Daimler CWA6 rebodied by Weymann in 1953, while on the right is DH389 (NKT 885), an all-Leyland PD2/12 new in 1951.
John Bishop / Online Transport Archive

Left: Stuart Road yard at Gravesend garage is the location for this view of DH82 (GKP 267), a 1944 Guy Arab rebodied by Weymann in 1952. New to M&D subsidiary Chatham & District, this vehicle had been transferred to the parent company in 1945. On the left is Beadle rebuild C369 (WKM 369), constructed in 1956 using components from AEC Regal III CO63 of 1949. *Howard Butler*

Above: In 1955 Chatham & District was absorbed into the parent company. One of a batch of eight vehicles delivered to Chatham & District in 1953, Weymann Orion-bodied Guy Arab IV DH452 (RKK 992) is pictured at Gillingham bus station in the early spring of 1968, by which time it was just weeks from withdrawal. Alongside is Weymann-bodied Leyland Atlantean 5501 (501 DKT), delivered in 1959 as DH501 and one of the initial batch of this type. How proud the fleetname looks on the garage behind. *John Bishop / Online Transport Archive*

17

Above: A fine nearside view of Weymann Orion-bodied Guy Arab IV DH459 (RKK 999), recorded at Gillingham bus station in the spring of 1968, the greatcoat worn by one of the staff giving an indication of the temperature. The silver roof, shown here to good advantage, would soon be history, as rear-loading buses were replaced in the late 1960s and early '70s. One wonders how much DH459's registration number would fetch on the open market if it were still available!
Malcolm Keeping

Right: Nearing the end of its life, DH470 (VKO 994), a 1955 Weymann Orion-bodied Guy Arab IV, seen in 1968 in Tunbridge Wells on route 7, which plied between Tunbridge Wells and Maidstone via Tonbridge. DH470 was one of a batch of eight ordered by Chatham & District; however, with the absorption into Maidstone & District in 1955 they were delivered in dark green and cream.
Malcolm Keeping

Left: In 1951 M&D took delivery of no fewer than 53 all-Leyland Titan PD2s. In 1954 more than half were fitted with platform doors, but DH382 (NKT 878), a highbridge PD2/12 model seen in Gillingham bus station in the spring of 1968, retained its open rear platform. Although still bearing its original fleet number it was by now officially 5382, having been renumbered 'on paper' in January. Upon withdrawal from the passenger fleet in 1970 this vehicle would become a driver-trainer (see page 78), in which form it would continue to serve the company until 1977. *Malcolm Keeping*

Above: Maidstone & District operated routes to Brighton jointly with Southdown. One of these was the 180, which took a very circuitous route from Hastings via Battle and Heathfield in East Sussex. Passing a Brighton, Hove & District Bristol KSW and a Southdown Leyland PD3/4 in Brighton's Old Steine, DH391 (NKT 887), an all-Leyland PD2/12 of 1951, nears journey's end at the town's Pool Valley bus station. *Howard Butler*

Left: Maidstone & District garages may not have been architectural delights, but the company nevertheless was proud of its heritage, as indicated by the company name on the roof of Hawkhurst garage, which was situated behind the town's bus station. Basking in sunshine in the spring of 1967 is DH380 (NKT 876), an all-Leyland PD2/12, behind which can be seen three more PD2s and a Harrington-bodied AEC Reliance, S254 (254 BKM), of 1958 vintage. *Dave Brown*

Above: A classic bus at a classic location. Having covered half its journey from Maidstone to Hastings, DH388 (NKT 884), an all-Leyland PD2/12 of 1951, takes a well-earned breather at Hawkhurst in the summer of 1967. The bus station still stands today and is the scene of many bus rallies. *Dave Brown*

Left: Leyland's 'Farington' body was as gracious from the rear as from the front, as apparent from this offside view of DH407 (NKT 903) at Tunbridge Wells Central station in the summer of 1967; note (on the nearside rear) the 'TW' plate denoting allocation to Tunbridge Wells garage. Heading in the opposite direction is Weymann Orion-bodied Bristol K6A DH120 (HKE 221) in its last weeks of service, while parked on the bridge over the Hastings–Charing Cross railway line is a Riley 4/72 Farina, which would nowadays be a favourite at any car rally. *Dave Brown*

Left: In the summer of 1968, when this view was recorded, all-Leyland PD2/12s were still plentiful, and it seemed as though they would last forever, but in two years they would be just a memory. In blissful ignorance of its impending fate, DH401 (NKT 897) basks in the sunshine outside St John's Road garage, Tunbridge Wells. Save for the buses and the Ford 105E Anglia, the scene is instantly recognisable today.. *John Bishop / Online Transport Archive*

Left: In 1953 the company took delivery of 20 Leyland PD2/12 Titans with rather austere-looking lightweight Weymann bodywork, as seen on DH433 (RKP 914) at Canterbury bus station. Although a number were renumbered in 1968 DH433 would not be among them, having been withdrawn in 1967. Route 67 was the 'main road' route from Maidstone to Canterbury. In this mid-1960s view Benson & Hedges cigarettes would cost the princely sum of just over 21 pence! *Howard Butler*

Below left: Opened in the 1950s, Canterbury bus station marked a leap forward for passengers and crews alike. It was always the preserve of the red buses of East Kent, such that Maidstone & District vehicles looked out of place. Ready for its 1½-hour trip back to Maidstone, DH422 (RKP 903), a Weymann Orion-bodied Leyland PD2/12 dating from 1953, looks pristine. The raised walkway behind provided an advantageous viewpoint for photography, but not this time! *Howard Butler*

Right: Photographed in Tunbridge Wells in the summer of 1967, Weymann Orion-bodied Leyland PD2/12 DH427 (RKP 908) of 1953 begins its descent of Mount Pleasant Road towards the town's Central station. Its ultimate destination is the 'West Station', which was to close many years later, when trains ceased to run to/from Uckfield. DH427, however, had a much shorter life expectancy and would be withdrawn (as 5427) in 1968. *Dave Brown*

Left: A fine offside view of 1953-built Weymann Orion-bodied Leyland Titan PD2/12 DH438 (RKP 919), recorded at Uckfield, East Sussex, in the mid-1960s. The exact location is Bell Lane, where the Southdown garage was located (and nowadays the link road from the A22 Uckfield by-pass to the town centre). The television station advertised on the offside has since been consigned to history, programmes on the ITV network now being provided locally by Meridian. *Malcolm Keeping*

Above: How more typically English can a street scene appear than in this view of the High Street in Charing? The timber-framed buildings on the left and later Victorian terraced houses on the right complement DH420 (RKP 901), photographed in the mid-1960s on the long trunk route (10) from Maidstone to Folkestone. The C-registered Triumph Vitesse appears almost new and would today be a treat in any car rally. *Howard Butler*

Above: In 1956 M&D turned to AEC for 22 Regent Vs, including DH477 (VKR 469), with highbridge Park Royal bodywork, pictured in Brighton's Old Steine. A frequent visitor to the Sussex coast, it is seen completing the long haul from Gravesend in Kent, which would have taken just over four hours. Taken in the mid-1960s, the photograph also features a Brighton Corporation Leyland PD2 with Weymann Orion bodywork — a combination also delivered to Maidstone & District in 1953/4. *Howard Butler*

Right: The seafront at Hastings is the setting for this nearside view of DH479 (VKR 471), another of the AEC Regent Vs with handsome Park Royal bodywork, on the inland route 15 to Eastbourne and looking just right with silver roof, light-green lining and red hubs on the wheels — plus, of course, the 'Dulux Du-Lite' advertisement so typical of buses in the 1950s and '60s. *A. P. Tatt / Online Transport Archive*

Above: Taken on a dismal day in the mid-1960s, this photograph depicts Park Royal-bodied AEC Regent V DH481 (VKR 473) pausing at Southdown's Uckfield bus station/garage before returning to Tunbridge Wells on route 79. Behind, and providing an interesting comparison, is a Southdown Guy Arab IV, also with Park Royal bodywork but to five-bay (rather than four-bay) construction, on service 192 to Eastbourne via Heathfield and Horam. *Malcolm Keeping*

Right: Of the 22 Park Royal-bodied AEC Regent Vs delivered in 1956, eight were of lowbridge layout. New as DL37, 6737 (VKR 37) is seen in Tonbridge on the A21 Pembury Road, about to turn left into M&D's recently built garage near the town centre. Looking absolutely pristine, the bus is being pursued by an early Ford Cortina and a Morris Minor 1000. Note on the left the traditional-style police station of the Kent Constabulary. *Malcolm Keeping*

Above: On 1 October 1957 M&D formally absorbed its Hastings Tramways subsidiary, and the trolleybuses were given 'Maidstone & District' fleetnames, as seen on No 8 (BDY 783), a Weymann-bodied AEC dating from 1940. Heading along the seafront in the opposite direction is a Weymann-bodied AEC Reliance of the East Kent Road Car Co, which ran services in this area from garages at Hastings and Rye. Within two years the Hastings trolleybus system would close, the trolleys being replaced in 1959 by M&D's first Leyland Atlanteans. *Rob Crouch collection*

Right: This view from the late 1950s features an immaculate Weymann-bodied Sunbeam W trolleybus, 37 (BDY 812), bound for Cooden Beach on route 8. Note the Maidstone & District fleetname and the customary advertisements applied to the front. The location is again Hastings seafront — a location changed little today save for the absence of the trolleybus infrastructure. Upon closure of the Hastings system in 1959, 37 would head north to Walsall Corporation, where it was to give another decade of valuable service. *A. P. Tatt / Online Transport Archive*

Above: From 1959, initially to replace Hastings' trolleybuses, came a massive influx of Leyland Atlanteans. Of the initial order for 50 delivered in 1959 14 had lowbridge bodywork by Weymann, including DL44 (44 DKT), seen in Bexhill on local route 156. The cars are a sight to behold, especially the Ford Consul Capri facing inland. *Rob Crouch*

Right: By 1962 Maidstone & District had the largest fleet of Atlanteans in the country, more than 100 having been delivered within three years. Their austere appearance was enhanced by the customary cream 'moustache' below the windscreen — a feature retained until NBC days. Carrying the inevitable *Kent Messenger* advertisements on either side of its destination screen, DH556 (556 LKP), one of the 1960 delivery with Metro-Cammell bodywork, stands in Maidstone's Lower Stone Street bus station ready for the run to Folkestone on route 10 (operated jointly with East Kent) in the summer of 1966. *Dave Brown*

Leyland Atlantean/Metro-Cammell DH573 (573 RKJ), delivered in 1961,
speeds up Bohemia Road, Hastings, with a full load on board on local route 133.
The photograph was taken from the Oval, where each May the Hastings Bus Rally
is held. *Malcolm Keeping*

In 1963 M&D changed allegiance yet again, following a batch of Weymann-bodied Atlanteans with its first examples of Daimler's recently introduced rival, the Fleetline, which chassis permitted a lower overall height. The company's first Daimlers since the war years, they also marked a return to Gardner engines — well-known for their reliability and longevity — but introduced a new bodybuilder, Northern Counties. New in 1964, DL62 (62 YKT) keeps company with a 1957 AEC Reliance/Weymann in Maidstone's Lower Stone Street bus station, both vehicles showing off the cream 'moustache' that was such a feature of M&D buses during this period. *Howard Butler*

Above: There is a saying among enthusiasts taking photographs of newly delivered vehicles that 'a bus is only new once'. Seen in Maidstone's Mill Street bus station when new in 1964, low-height Northern Counties-bodied Daimler Fleetline DL61 (61 YKT) is flanked by a pair of Leyland PD2s while on layover between journeys on local route 139. The embellishers fitted to the front and rear wheels certainly added a touch of class befitting the name of Daimler, so long associated with luxury cars. *Malcolm Keeping*

Right: When this photograph was taken in 1968 DL80 (80 YKT) was only four years old but had lost much of its elegance. By now officially 6080, it is seen outside St John's Road garage, Tunbridge Wells, in conditions perfect for photography. Fremlins, the virtues of which are extolled in the advertisement, was very much a Kent brew and was much respected by real-ale enthusiasts. *John Bishop / Online Transport Archive*

Above: The combination of Bristol L-type chassis and Eastern Coach Works body was very much a Tilling Group standard. Upon the formation of the British Transport Commission (BTC) after World War 2 sales were restricted to BTC companies, although Bristol and ECW were permitted to fulfill orders that had been placed before nationalisation. Into this category came a number of vehicles delivered to M&D in 1950, including SO56 (MKN 205), an example of the lengthened LL5G version, with five-cylinder Gardner engine, seen on Tonbridge local route 132 in the early 1960s. *Malcolm Keeping*

Right: In 1951/2 M&D took delivery of 40 Beadle 'chassisless' coaches constructed using parts from withdrawn prewar AEC Regents. This view at the Cooden Beach terminus of trolleybus route 8 features SO98 (NKT 957); 'new' in 1951 as CO229, it was converted for bus work early in 1955 and finished in this attractive dark-green livery. The passing Rover and fashions of the late 1950s complete the scene. *A. P. Tatt / Online Transport Archive*

The ever-popular location of St John's Road garage, Tunbridge Wells, is the setting for this view of SO68 (RKE 540), the Saunders-Roe integral bus delivered in 1953. It was renumbered (as S68) in 1961, so the photograph showing the vehicle with its original fleet number, most probably dates from the late 1950s.

With its horizontal five-cylinder Gardner engine and semi-chassisless construction it would always be the odd man out but looked stylish nevertheless with the M&D scroll affixed to the bodyside. *Malcolm Keeping*

The Weymann body also looked quite stylish in Maidstone & District livery, and the combination of this and the AEC Reliance chassis, favoured for single-deckers from 1956, made for a very dependable machine. This mid-1960s photograph shows S216 (XKT 993), new in 1957 as SO216, waiting to leave Maidstone's Lower Stone Street bus station on route 29 to Chatham. Certain journeys were extended to Gillingham. *Malcolm Keeping*

Above: An unusually deserted Mount Pleasant Road in Tunbridge Wells is the setting for this April 1968 view of S235 (YKR 235), an AEC Reliance bodied by Beadle of Dartford. By 1957, when this vehicle was delivered, Beadle was nearing the end of its bodybuilding activities, so it is fitting that another of this batch, S224, should be preserved by an enthusiast based in East Sussex.
John Bishop / Online Transport Archive

Right: Albion was a marque normally associated with Scottish operators, so it came as a surprise in the late 1950s and early '60s to see examples of its small, lightweight Nimbus model appearing in the South, M&D taking 15 in 1960. Bodied by Thomas Harrington of Hove, East Sussex, these vehicles proved ideal for lightly trafficked routes. New as SO317, 3317 (317 LKK) is seen in Pembury Road, Tonbridge, towards the end of its M&D career; withdrawn in 1970, it would end up in Hong Kong. *Malcolm Keeping*

Operated jointly with the East Kent Road Car Co, route 67 from Maidstone to Canterbury could boast an hourly service along the main A20 road and was very much a flagship route for both operators. Here S347 (347 NKT), a 1961

AEC Reliance with dual-purpose Weymann bodywork, disgorges its passengers in Canterbury bus station at the end of the 1½-hour journey. A professional touch is provided by the green-painted wheel-embellishers. *Howard Butler*

Between May 1962 and May 1969 S335 (335 NKT), a dual-purpose Weymann-bodied AEC Reliance of 1961, wore this smart livery. The boat-rack seen in this view recorded on Brighton's Madeira Drive was fitted in February 1967 but would be removed in September 1970 following problems encountered in tilt-testing.
Malcolm Keeping

Left: In 1962 Maidstone & District took delivery of a 36ft AEC Reliance 590 with bodywork by Willowbrook of Loughborough, a builder hitherto unrepresented in the fleet save by a couple of second-hand acquisitions prewar. Exhibited prior to delivery at the 1962 Commercial Motor Show, S1 (984 TKO) had seating for 54 passengers, which represented a huge increase in capacity for a single-deck bus. Looking immaculate in the spring sunshine in the late 1960s, it appears to be the subject of staff conversation at St John's Road garage, Tunbridge Wells. *Malcolm Keeping*

Above: In 1963 Maidstone & District took delivery of four more 36ft Willowbrook-bodied AEC Reliances, S2-5 (2-5 YKK). The extra length stretched the driver's skills when negotiating a sharp turn, as can be seen from this mid-1960s view of S2 (2 YKK) in Tonbridge on local route 100. *Malcolm Keeping*

51

Left: As the 1960s progressed Maidstone & District, along with many other operators, continued to favour the AEC Reliance for its single-deck requirements. In 1965 the company took delivery of further 590-type chassis, this time with bodywork by Marshall of Cambridge — a combination represented here by S6 (BKT 821C), at the entrance to the lower level of Tunbridge Wells garage when still quite new. Built to standard design, the vehicle is enhanced by M&D's superb livery, which gave the traditional air of quality so long associated with the company. *Malcolm Keeping*

Above: A new chassis type delivered to Maidstone & District in 1965 was the Leyland Panther, with engine located at the rear instead of under the floor within the wheelbase, as was by this time the norm for single-deckers. Willowbrook-bodied S28 (DKE 253C) stands proudly in Maidstone's Mill Street bus station when almost new, giving no hint of the reliability problems the type would suffer in their early years. Renumbered 3028 in 1968, this example would nevertheless serve the company for 12 years, surviving until 1977. *Malcolm Keeping*

Above: Out with the old and in with the new. Standing in Maidstone's Mill Street bus station when brand-new in 1967, Leyland Panther/Willowbrook S108 (JKK 208E) makes for an interesting contrast with all-Leyland PD2/12 DH386 (NKT 882) of 1951. Although the Panthers were to earn themselves a somewhat dubious reputation there is no denying how handsome they looked in M&D's traditional livery, which still retained the 'moustache' below the windscreen and scroll fleetname. This example would enjoy a relatively short life with the company, becoming nominally a Wilts & Dorset bus (though owned by Hants & Dorset) in July 1972. *Dave Brown*

Right: Brand-new Leyland Panther/Willowbrook S109 (JKK 209E) is seen making its way along Hastings seafront in the summer of 1967 on the lengthy route 12 to Maidstone via Tenterden. Renumbered 3109 the following year, it would be among 33 such vehicles transferred in 1971/2 to Hants & Dorset, this particular example donning Wilts & Dorset red livery. *Dave Brown*

In 1968 M&D turned to Strachans to body a further batch of 30 Leyland Panthers, represented here by 3122 (LKT 122F) in Maidstone's Mill Street bus station in August 1968. Quite different in styling from the standard BET Federation design produced by the likes of Marshall and Willowbrook, the bodywork on these vehicles marked a refreshing change but was to prove structurally troublesome, requiring extensive rebuilding in the early 1970s. *Howard Butler*

In 1969/70 M&D received 30 Daimler Fleetline single-deckers with dual-door bodywork by Marshall. Delivered in the company's traditional livery, complete with scroll fleetnames, they were attractive vehicles but were destined to have short lives with M&D; a dozen were soon transferred to Northern General in exchange for a similar number of double-deck Fleetlines, whilst others stayed closer to home, with Alder Valley (whence they too would ultimately migrate to Northern) and East Kent. Seen when still quite new, 3822 (SKO 822H) would be transferred to the latter in July 1977 for use on Seaspeed services at Dover. *Malcolm Keeping*

Left: A tranquil early-1970s scene at Penshurst which encapsulates the heyday of Maidstone & District. Taking centre stage is 3417 (UKE 417H), one of the first batch of short Leyland Leopard buses delivered in the spring of 1970, its Marshall body featuring such refinements as aluminium beading, twin headlights and chrome bumpers. In the distance is a Harrington-bodied AEC Reliance coach.The bus-stop sign is of a style unique to M&D, while the generous shelter serves as a meeting-place for friends to catch up while waiting for the bus. *Rob Crouch*

Above: The second of 16 Leyland Leopard buses delivered in the summer of 1972, 3442 (EKJ 442K) is seen when new outside the offices of the erstwhile Hastings Tramways Co at Silverhill garage, St Leonards-on-Sea. Lacking the refinements seen on 3417 opposite, its Marshall body is nevertheless enhanced by M&D's traditional livery. Note the lone trolleybus traction pole standing defiantly on the left. *Rob Crouch*

Left: Seen on Madeira Drive, Brighton, on the occasion of the London–Brighton run of 2 May 1965 is an absolute classic in the shape of Harrington-bodied Leyland Tiger TS7 CO558 (DKT 16). New in 1937 (as 58), it had been rebodied by the original coachbuilder in 1950, its new body incorporating a full-length roof-rack for the carriage of band instruments. In this form it continued to serve M&D for a further 14 years, being sold for preservation just six months before the picture was taken. Thankfully it is still with us today. *Malcolm Keeping*

Above: At one time there were three garages in Hastings — two for the trolleybuses and one (Brook Street) for Maidstone & District buses. The tram tracks and the presence behind of 1928 trolleybus No 3 'Happy Harold' reveal that this early-1960s photograph was taken at the one-time Hastings tramways depot at Silverhill. Peering out at the sunshine is CO116 (KKK 855), numerically the last of the batch of full-fronted Harrington-bodied AEC Regal III coaches of 1949. Withdrawn in 1963, this vehicle was to end its days in Cornwall. *Malcolm Keeping*

Above: Mention Skinner's today in Hastings or St Leonards-on-Sea and the populace will recognise the firm as a car dealer, failing to recall the coach operator of pre- and early postwar years. The company was acquired on 15 August 1953 along with a fleet of coaches including C122 (FDY 246), depicted at Brook Street garage, Hastings, in the early 1960s. A Gurney Nutting-bodied AEC Regal IV delivered in June 1952, it would last until 1965. *Malcolm Keeping*

Above right: In 1952 M&D took delivery of its first underfloor-engined coaches, in the shape of 15 Leyland Royal Tigers. All but one were bodied by Leyland itself, the odd man out being CO272 (PKE 272), a Harrington-bodied example exhibited

at the 1952 Commercial Motor Show. Collectors of Dinky Toy models will recognise the styling as that of the blue BOAC coach marketed in the late 1950s/early '60s (and now highly collectable). *Malcolm Keeping*

Right: Harrington coachwork, albeit to a modified design, was fitted in 1953/4 to a further 14 Royal Tigers, including CO293 (SKE 989), seen at the rear of Silverhill garage in the early 1960s. Delivered in March 1954 and withdrawn in 1965, it would no doubt represent a shrewd purchase for its next owner, a London-based contractor. *Malcolm Keeping*

The AEC Reliance would be M&D's standard coach for many years, based upon experience with the initial batch of 37-seat Harrington Wayfarer-bodied vehicles, including CO341 (TKM 341) delivered in 1955. By now officially 4341, it is seen at Gillingham garage in the spring of 1968, shortly before withdrawal.
John Bishop / Online Transport Archive

One could be forgiven for not paying closer attention to what at first glance appears to be just another Harrington Wayfarer-bodied AEC or Leyland. In fact C351 (TKM 351) was a Harrington Contender integral coach fitted with a Commer TS3 two-stroke diesel engine. New in 1955, it was one of three such machines which lasted in service until 1966 and gave fine service in the intervening years. It is seen in the mid-1960s at Brighton's Race Hill, where many gems could be found. *Malcolm Keeping*

A chance look inside Southdown's garage at Uckfield in the early 1960s prompted this 'couldn't resist' photograph of 'chassisless' Beadle-AEC CO361 (WKM 361), a 1955 rebuild using parts from AEC Regal III CO62, new in 1948 with prewar Harrington coachwork. In rebuilt form it would serve M&D for a further nine years, not being withdrawn until 1964. *Malcolm Keeping*

Harrington's Wayfarer body evolved as the 1950s progressed, culminating in the Wayfarer IV, which design became particularly associated with Maidstone & District, on AEC Reliance 470 chassis. The 1957 coach intake comprised 13 such vehicles, including CO382 (382 BKM), seen on Hastings seafront while on a 'South Downs Tour' in the mid-1960s. By now this vehicle had been renumbered C382, the 'O' — signifying oil (diesel) engine — having been dropped in 1961. *Rob Crouch*

Seen outside the lower level of Tunbridge Wells garage in April 1968, Harrington Wayfarer-bodied AEC Reliance SC391 (391 DKK) started life in 1958 as coach CO391 but was renumbered in 1963 upon rebuilding with a normal saloon front. As a result of the rebuild it could be used on both stage-carriage and coach duties, but it never looked quite right in this form. The vehicle would be renumbered twice more — as 2391 in 1968 and as 3361 in 1971. Note the angular lines of the classic Triumph Renown motor car on the right. *John Bishop / Online Transport Archive*

Of 20 AEC Reliance/Harrington coaches new in 1960, two were delivered in Skinner's blue livery while a third — CO444 (444 LKE) — arrived in Scout red and cream. By the time this photograph was taken at Brook Street garage in Hastings this vehicle had been renumbered C444; renumbered again (as 4444) in 1968, it would adopt M&D colours in 1969 (having been the last coach in Scout livery), before succumbing to NBC leaf-green bus livery (as 3204) in 1974. *Rob Crouch*

Left: The British Coach Rally was the opportunity for any self-respecting operator to show off its latest coaches, Maidstone & District being no exception. Seen on Brighton's Madeira Drive in May 1963 is C29 (29 TKR), a Harrington Cavalier-bodied AEC Reliance delivered in October of the previous year but stored pending the start of the coaching season. With a certain bias the writer reckons this to be the zenith of coach design and of livery application, representing the true heyday of Maidstone & District. *John Bishop / Online Transport Archive*

Above: Coaches tend to be among the more elusive vehicles to capture on film, forcing the photographer to resort to garage locations. This mid-1960s view inside Knightrider Street garage, Maidstone, features SC31 (31 YKK), one of a pair of dual-purpose Willowbrook-bodied AEC Reliance 590s delivered in 1963. In the 1968 renumbering SC31 would become 2531. *Malcolm Keeping*

Left: Located in Quarry Hill Road near its junction with Hastings Road, M&D's Tonbridge garage was opened as late as 1961. In the afternoon its forecourt was ideal for photography, as demonstrated by this view of 4155 (AKP 252B), a Harrington Grenadier-bodied AEC Reliance 590. New in 1964 as C35 and renumbered in 1968, it was to have a woefully short life, being destroyed by fire in 1972. *Rob Crouch*

Above: New as C72, 4172 (FKL 135D) was the last numerically of a batch of 15 Harrington Grenadier-bodied AEC Reliance 590s delivered in the autumn of 1965 but stored unused until the spring of 1966. This handsome coach is seen negotiating The Square in Bournemouth in the late 1960s. Note the overhead wiring for the town's trolleybuses, which would shortly follow those of Hastings into oblivion. *Rob Crouch*

Basking in the sun outside St John's Road garage, Tunbridge Wells, in the spring of 1968 is SC52 (BKT 815C), a dual-purpose Weymann-bodied AEC Reliance 590, one of 20 such vehicles delivered in 1965. Three years old when photographed (and by now officially 2552), it would be physically renumbered later in the year.

Behind is Harrington-bodied AEC Reliance S263 (263 BKM), while in front is a bumper-less Ford Prefect with 'go faster' decal on the grille!
John Bishop / Online Transport Archive

Right: Mill Street bus station, Maidstone, in the spring of 1965, as brand-new Weymann-bodied AEC Reliance SC55 (BKT 818C) waits to depart on the express service to London. The coach-seated (but bus-liveried) Reliance on the left carries an 'EXPRESS SERVICE' board, suggesting that it will serve as a duplicate if required. *Malcolm Keeping*

Below right: The BET Federation body design, built by Marshall, Weymann and Willowbrook, was used for bus and dual-purpose vehicles alike. This photograph, taken in Maidstone's Knightrider Street garage *c*1970 provides a comparison of Marshall-bodied AEC Reliances. Taking centre stage is dual-purpose 2574 (HKR 174D), delivered in 1966 as SC74, while on the right is bus 3720 (BKT 835C), new in 1965 as S20. Just in view on the left is Weymann-bodied 2555 (BKT 818C), new in 1965 as SC55. *Malcolm Keeping*

75

In 1968 Maidstone & District turned to the Leyland Leopard, although the AEC Reliance would continue in production for years to come. Having proved itself with many other operators, the underfloor-engined Leopard was a dependable chassis, suitable for bus or coach bodywork. M&D's first examples were a dozen coaches, the Duple Commander III bodywork making for a very attractive vehicle, as apparent from this view of 4607 (NKL 207F) at Maidstone garage when new. *Malcolm Keeping*

Later in 1968 M&D took delivery of a further batch of 18 Leopards, with handsome dual-purpose Willowbrook bodywork. Seen at Hastings' Brook Street garage when relatively new, 2813 (OKO 813G) has blinds set for the lengthy route 5 from Maidstone, for which this type of vehicle was ideally suited. Happily sister vehicle 2816 survives in preservation and can be seen at rallies throughout the South of England. *Rob Crouch*

Left: The service fleet of most operators held much interest, and Maidstone & District was no exception. Seen outside Brook Street garage, Hastings, all-Leyland PD2/12 702 (NKT 878) had been new in 1951 as DH382; renumbered as 5382 in 1968, it was converted as a driver-trainer in September 1970 and painted in this smart livery of green with red waistband and silver roof. Further renumbered in 1973 as P2, it would serve in this role until 1976. *Malcolm Keeping*

Left: Seen in Maidstone High Street in December 1975, driver-trainer P3 (VKR 469), a Park Royal-bodied AEC Regent V new as DH477 in 1956, makes its way past Maidstone Corporation 23 (23 YKO), a Massey-bodied Leyland PD2. Converted for driver training in October 1971, it was initially renumbered as 703, becoming P3 in January 1973 and surviving thus until October 1976. *John Bishop / Online Transport Archive*

Right: Taken at Southdown's Uckfield garage, this atmospheric photograph appears to depict a Maidstone & District takeover! Bristol K6A/Weymann DH122 (HKE 223) is being rescued by breakdown lorry E2, an AEC Matador new in 1940 to the Ministry of Defence and acquired by M&D for conversion as a recovery vehicle in 1961. *Malcolm Keeping*

Right: Seen beneath the trolleybus wires in Knightrider Street, Maidstone, in the summer of 1967 is Leyland TD4 No 310 (CKO 988). New in 1936 as bus 310, it had its original double-deck Weymann body replaced in 1950 by the 1936 Harrington lorry body (with a crane and an ambulance section at the rear) originally fitted to Leyland TD1 805 (KP 3400) of 1929. Thankfully this most interesting of vehicles survives today in preservation. *Dave Brown*

79

No book on Maidstone & District would be complete without a view of Knightrider House. By July 1977, when this photograph was taken, DH400 (NKT 896), an all-Leyland Titan PD2/12, had been withdrawn seven years and was now preserved by the photographer. Happily the bus was allowed to venture back onto M&D property to be photographed outside the building where so many decisions were taken affecting public transport in Kent and East Sussex. *Dave Brown*